The Revealing

The Execution to the Masquerade

LATISHA R. MITCHELL

TABLE OF CONTENTS

1   Hidden Figures, Filthy Roots   11

2   Identifying The Foreign Intruders   15

3   Help Me, I've Fallen and It's Hard For ME To Get Up   23

4   The Me That's Overtaken By Them   31

5   When You Love Them More Than   39

6   Grabbing The Pieces Of ME   47

7   ME vs ME   53

8   Facing The Raw Facts   59

9   Reform to Conform   67

10   Damaged Goods Still Holds The Goods   71

11   Now That The Masquerade Is Over   77

12   The Reveal   81

  End to Begin   87

ACKNOWLEDGEMENTS

I would first like to give honor to the Father, who has allowed me to share my story. My earnest prayer and heart's desire is that this book will uplift and inspire someone as they read this book. I'm thankful for all that God has brought me through and what He has allowed me to overcome. I don't regret anything that has taken place in these last 38 years of my life. I'm forever grateful for all that the Father has bestowed upon me, and I'm humbled that He would allow me to be a vessel He could use to help others. Here's to you, Daddy, for always being there and never leaving me; when I felt alone or wanting to be left alone. I love you with my whole heart. Forever your Daughter.

To My Son, Paulzair A. Alston, and Daughter, Promise J. Mitchell: You all are what help my heart to beat and keep me pressing forward. I'm so blessed to have a set of children that God has gifted me with. I pray that my life and my accomplishments in life will make you all smile and be very proud that I'm your mother. Everything I do, Paulzair and Promise, is for you guys. Words could never express how much

I love you guys; I wish you could see my heart; you all are right there in the center. Mom loves you both.

To My Mother, Evangelist Julia Myzick-Watkins: Thanks for birthing me into the world and raising me in the church and introducing me to Jesus. Thank you for all your many sacrifices to raise Matthew and I. You always have been an example of a woman of God to myself and others. I love you very much, and I wouldn't be the woman of God I have become without you, thank you! I hope I make you very proud of me.

To My Father, James W. Lee: I want you to know that I love you very much and I pray that I will make you proud. Thanks for being there when you could, and I'm glad God has allowed you to father me.

To My Second Mother, Apostle Dr. T.L Penny: Thank you so much, for loving me and allowing me to be in your life. Mommy, thank you for the many impartations and seeing greatness in me. I love you very much, and I'm grateful to God for blessing me with you. You hold a special place in my heart, and you are irreplaceable. My Heart Forever.

To My Aunt and Spiritual Mother, Pastor Avis Frasier: Thank you so very much for always pouring into me over these last twenty-four years and encouraging me. Thank you for always being a listening ear and always giving sound, Godly advice. I love you very much!

To My Siblings: Darron, Helyn, Angie, Trent, and Matthew: Hey, I love you guys very much, and I pray that I will make all of you proud. You all are the best, and I'm glad that we are siblings.

To My Family and Close Friends: I thank God for all of you. Thank you all for the encouragement and the times you've been there for my children and I. You all are greatly appreciated. I love you all very much.

Special Thanks To Apostle Aaron Mobley, Jr. I thank God for you and how God has divinely connected us. Thank you so much for all your help and for pushing me into even greater things. You have been such a blessing and an inspiration to many and myself. You most definitely are an Apostolic General in the Kingdom! Thank you for everything, Apostle, and multiple mega blessings to you and your family!

LATISHA R. MITCHELL

INTRODUCTION

Ever since I was a little girl, I've always faced many difficult challenges. I was born with a heart condition that will always keep me limited when it comes to achieving my dreams. Things like going into the Air Force or playing pro basketball; with my aortic valve leaking and me having a heart murmur, these childhood desires were quickly shattered as time progressed. I was born on July 3, 1980 and my mother named me Latisha Rene'e Myzick; she said she wanted to name me Zeltisha, which I'm so glad she didn't! My family calls me Nae-Nae for short which they took from my middle name, Rene'e. As a single mother raising my brother and I, my mother did the best she could. We didn't have an excellent or exciting childhood as some children might have had, but I can say that my mother worked hard, and we always had the best she could offer materially and never lacked the necessities to survive.

My mother raised my brother Matthew and I in the church. I gave my life to Jesus on November 22, 1989, in Hartford, Connecticut, at Gospel Lighthouse Apostolic Church, which marked my first life-changing journey with Christ. My mother sometimes would send my brother and I to my father and our older siblings in Connecticut. I love my father, don't get me wrong, but I must be totally honest and say he wasn't the best dad he could have been while my brother and I were growing up. So, this caused me not to be the best daughter I could be, the best young lady I could be, and knowing my worth. A father should want to be that young girl's best friend, protector, and even first perfect male role model for her to see. I didn't have that, I was thinking that the men that I would give my body away to, not being my husband was the best for me. Having an absentee father in my life caused me so much added pain and self-inflicted wounds. However, I never knew that my father not being present in the home or in my life, would trigger a domino effect that would lead to some of my greatest, most painful downfalls in life. I wouldn't realize the root of the rejection that caused hurt along with the repeated cycles, because of a little girl who felt unloved and unwanted by her father, until July of 2018 -- when I was in yet another toxic relationship. This continuous root of hurt that was never dealt with and chopped completely down, created the Masquerade face that often covered the real Latisha. I became isolated and buried alive underneath the harsh burden of wanting to be loved, but never being able to truly receive love, especially in a romantic relationship.

While reading this book that mostly will reveal the hidden me, I pray that it will illuminate someone and motivate some of you to pursue healing and restoration for your life. You're not what you were in the past, who they once called you or not even what you sometimes may think or feel about yourself negatively. Our God thinks more highly of you than you could ever imagine. You're so perfect to Him, and when He made you, He called you good! Therefore, all things are working for your good as well. One of God's Love Letters to Us say, "For I know the thoughts that I think toward you, saith the Lord, thoughts of peace, and not of evil, to give you an expected end." Jeremiah 29:11.

The Father is crazy in love with you and me! He loves you beyond your failures or mishaps that have occurred or will occur in your life. I pray that while reading this book, that you become healed, whole and restored.

LATISHA R. MITCHELL

1

HIDDEN FIGURES, FILTHY ROOTS

"Behold, I was shapen in iniquity; and in sin did my mother conceive me. Behold, thou desirest truth in the inward parts: and in the hidden part thou shalt make me to know wisdom. Purge me with hyssop, and I shall be clean: wash me, and I shall be whiter than snow." **Psalms 51:5-7**

My innocent girlhood was quickly violated, while at my Godmother's house at the age of five, asking for some toilet tissue and my Godmother's son came into the bathroom and molested me. He warned me not to tell anyone or I would get a whipping. I held it in until the age of seven, at which point I would experience yet another encounter that was a violation, but this time it was a close relative who was watching my brother and I until my mother got off from work. Almost every day when he was over to watch us, while my brother was asleep, he would fondle me and I remember him taking some water, and spitting it on my private parts, I guess because I wasn't getting moist enough. When I finally broke my silence and told my mother, this caused friction in the family and instilled a great fear in me to be left alone with any male figures at all. I wish not to disclose which family members violated me. However, another family member who is even closer than these others, came to stay with us one summer when I was nine years old, and would come into my room and inappropriately touch my body as well. It wasn't until the age of twenty-seven that I would finally tell my mother.

These next two incidents that occurred I thought I would never recover from; it took me several years for healing to take place. One summer I was at a friend's house and she had some boys over who were much older than us. One of them came into the room where I was watching television. He was nineteen years old and he took my virginity. I had no clue of what to do. I thought my menstruation had come on, because the others never entered my vagina; they just played with me and over me. So, me yet being young and ignorant to everything, the girl told me "don't say anything, or we will both get in trouble!" Well, not too long after the incident, I had to say something, because it could no longer remain a secret. I ended up pregnant at the age of eleven in the fifth grade and having a stillborn and throwing the baby in the dumpster. I initially hid it from my mother, but later had to reveal it at school in front of my mother, teacher, and my principal. It was one of the hardest thing I would ever have to go through, or so I thought! A few years later at the age of thirteen, I was raped yet again, this time by a pastor that I trusted and looked up to as a father. Right there at that very moment, I had given up on my life and I said what the hey; I guess I'm only good for sex.

You would think, after all I had been through, that I would give up on men or hate them, but instead I became very promiscuous. I started lying to my mother and telling her I'm at this or that person's house, but really I was with a guy who was much older than me. I told myself I loved them, but they surely didn't feel the same. Throughout the years, I would try to find someone who would be able to fill the void of rejection, and I just wanted to be loved. This was only the beginning that I would allow men, to have the pieces of me… until it became so very hard for me to even collect what was mine and what belongs to me. My birth given right was taken from me; yes, actually at birth, because I didn't know my worth and who I really was chosen to be. I lost all my goods and without the Father, I would have lost my mind as well. Years would come and go before I realized that only God can fill the void that I had. It would be years as well, before I allowed Him to heal me and restore me to my rightful state and cause me to become whole, healthy and established. I had an issue that plagued me constantly and left me broken and in a state of depression, but I'm grateful that I finally gave the brokenness of my life and heart over to the One who could put me back together again. Besides, He's the One that made Latisha in the first place. I am here to report that God can do the same for you, as He has done for me.

2

IDENTIFYING THE WELCOMED INTRUDERS

"Put on the whole armour of God, that ye may be able to stand against the wiles of the devil. For we wrestle not against flesh and blood, but against principalities, against powers, against the rulers of the darkness of this world, against spiritual wickedness in high places. Wherefore take unto you the whole armour of God, that ye may be able to withstand in the evil day, and having done all, to stand." **Ephesians 6:11-13**

Sometimes during the summer when I was younger, my mother would send my brother and I to my aunt's house down in Enterprise, Alabama. Mark being the first guy that I loved and gave my body to freely, would also be the guy who would hurt me and cause me to discover the vengeful personality, that I myself never knew was locked away deep down inside of me, waiting for her opportunity to venture and act out. I met him at the Greyhound station on my way to Alabama. He would become the first guy I thought really loved me, but no, it wasn't love at all. I was naïve to think a twenty-six year old and fifteen year old, would work out. In 1996, I went to Atlanta to surprise him on Valentine's Day; my cousin and myself drove there. He had given me a key to his place, because I would sneak out and drive there often. Yes, me driving to Atlanta at that age, because I got my first car at fifteen years old, a red Mustang GT to be exact. However, when I got there this time, Mark had another woman in his house. Me being young, I lost my temper and I cut him on his arm and then drove him to the hospital. I felt low and disheartened by this, because I thought he really loved me. But I lost the love I had for myself, as I continued seeking the love I didn't receive from my father and I continued feeling unloved and unwanted by mother. For many years, I had consistently been repeating the same cycles. It wasn't until I became sick of me and tired of my unhealthy and sinful ways that I would ultimately change.

Many times, we invite or allow people into our lives, for one reason or another. Oftentimes, we will allow these people to set a precedent in our lives; they all have different smiles, different names and different faces, but in most instances they carry the same actions. We begin to give them time, perhaps show them affection and even become loyal to them. Some of these people may live in our homes, and we have intimate relationships with them. Some may be people who we work with at our jobs and we befriended them, while others we may have met by just passing by in the street, a shopping mall, maybe a sports game or in a restaurant. At first the relationship is grand, everything is just peaches and cream, until one day the mask comes off of that person that you put trust in, because you felt as though you built some type of relationship by spending time together. Time that you can't ever get back; all of a sudden, you begin to ask yourself, who is this person? What was I thinking? How did I get myself here? You have allowed an intruder into your life, and then they became a close acquaintance; sometimes too close. Merriam-Webster defines Intruder as- *To thrust or force in or upon someone or something especially without permission, welcome, or fitness.* However, the individuals we allowed into our personal space were invited and they had our permission and there was no forced entry. We welcomed them in and they were perfect and innocent until they were proven wrong by what they may have said or done. That is why it is so vitally important to be careful who we freely give our hearts to, as well as our time. We must not be so open to trust people automatically. Everyone you meet you should put on "probation," no exceptions. We should never give people total access to us, trusting them with the one heart we have and were given to circulate blood, which causes a beat and gives us the vital functions to be able to live.

That is why the word of God says, "Trust in the lord with all thine heart, and lean not to your own understanding. In all thy ways acknowledge him, and he will direct thy paths." Proverbs 3:5-6. Let's be completely honest and examine ourselves... shall we? We don't at times trust the Father with all our hearts, because we oftentimes in our human nature try to play God, by fixing things and people that we believe can be salvaged. We really don't give God our broken and damaged situations at first. We first try to fix it ourselves, mend it ourselves or even get rid of it ourselves! Sometimes we get tired waiting on God, and we often have a microwaveable mentality that I want it now and hurry up. The Bible declares, "Wait on the LORD: be of good courage, and he shall strengthen thine heart: wait, I say, on the LORD." Psalms 27:14. We must not be in haste, because we will miss what God may want to do in our lives during the process of the waiting period. The wait is always for our own good and has a saving purpose. If I had waited, it would have saved me from heartaches or disappointments. Don't get tired in the wait.

Even when you become tired in your wait, the Bible declares, "But they that wait upon the Lord shall renew their strength; they shall mount up with wings as eagles; they shall run, and not be weary; and they shall walk, and not faint."

If you move too fast or grow weary and make haste, you aren't giving yourself enough time to develop and grow a pair of strong wings like eagles. To soar you must be willing to learn the "Present of Waiting". We must remember that at times it may seem as though the Father is taking too long to come to our rescue or even to answer us, but we must learn that there are wonderful unforeseen presents that comes with waiting. A lot of hurtful and painful situations would have been avoided if we had prayed and waited. The Bible says, "Be careful for nothing; but in everything by prayer and supplication with thanksgiving let your requests be made known unto God." Philippians 4:6. Beloved, because we don't pray and wait this causes a downward spiral that is hard to become uplifted out of and able to climb out of. All because we don't like to wait, until we sometimes find ourselves almost half dead when we finally are ready to say, "Here, God, you know what's best for me," and right about now after you've made a huge mess, now you're crying to God, "Here, here, I'm to pooped out to put up another fight...save me!"

We often don't pray about those who we allow into our space and who we give our precious time to, which we can't ever get back ever! We must learn to evaluate everything and pray about anyone that we may come in contact with and ask the Father why is this happening? Why have I met this person? Please note, singles, that everyone we come in contact with and meet, is not a person who we must date! If we were to acknowledge God truly and ask Him to direct our paths, this will save so many of us from becoming hurt or trying to play a mini Savior; which none of us are qualified to do. At the end of the day, WE are the ones who need saving from our own messed up destructive ways and habits that keep on attracting welcomed intruders into our personal space and lives. We must come to a point in our lives where we put up a No Trespassing sign to keep the intruders out, but let's make sure that we aren't removing the sign for those who we think look like they are innocent or appealing to our eyes or flesh. "Two of the most dangerous weaknesses to any human, the lust of the eye and lust of the flesh. For I know that in me (that is, in my flesh) dwelleth no good thing: for to will is present with me; but how to perform that which is good I find not." Romans 7:18.

Our eyes and minds play a major trick on us and because of that, it causes self-inflicted wounds and also self-destruction. It causes so much damage until sometimes it takes years and years to recover. However, I'm here to encourage you; you shall recover all, just as I have! It doesn't take God a long time to deliver us from our situations or circumstances, however, it takes us a long time to want to be delivered from the biggest enemy, which is your inner You! People must become tired of themselves in order to want to give up themselves for a burning sacrifice that will become whole and holy before the Father. The Scripture states, "I beseech you therefore, brethren, by the mercies of God, that ye present your bodies a living sacrifice, holy, acceptable unto God, which is your reasonable service. And be not conformed to this world: but be ye transformed by the renewing of your mind, that ye may prove what is that good, and acceptable, and perfect, will of God." Romans 12:1-2.

You must allow the Father to burn up those things that are not pleasing in His sight. It's not enough to say, "I'm going to repent" and then there be no change. To repent means to turn and go the opposite direction of which you were once traveling. You can be in this world, but not of the world. You must continue to renew your mind daily. You must consistently feed your spirit with the word of God. We must pray without ceasing and also pray and continue to ask the Father to please make us better. You must feed your spirit in order for your flesh to die. You must change your appetite from the things that make your flesh feel good to things that will feed your spirit and cause it to grow and become strong and win much warfare! Whatever you give the most nutrients to, will stand with the most strength and we wouldn't fall into divers temptations so easily. We become properly fit to win against temptations when we read our Bible, pray and fast. In order to live, you must kill what is trying to kill you, which is your flesh.

3

Help Me, I Have Fallen And It's Hard For Me To Get Up

"Wherefore seeing we also are compassed about with so great a cloud of witnesses, let us lay aside every weight, and the sin which doth so easily beset us, and let us run with patience the race that is set before us, Looking unto Jesus the author and finisher of our faith; who for the joy that was set before him endured the cross, despising the shame, and is set down at the right hand of the throne of God." **Hebrews 12: 1-2**

Men, Men, and More Men! A harlot in the church! Going to church, but the church wasn't in me. "Having a form of godliness, but denying the power thereof: from such turn away." 2 Timothy 3:5 Some are addicted to drugs or alcohol, I was addicted to sex and the men who could give it to me! This same addiction would later get me in more trouble than I would be able to get out of, long with losing precious time from my life. I knew I had a problem, when I couldn't go without sex for more than thirty days, no lie. Thank God for total deliverance. This was a deep rooted spirit of fornication that controlled my life. Yes, this same young lady that got saved in 1989 was operating in the church and fornicating. Now I wasn't preaching, just yet mainly playing the drums and doing some praise and worship; oh, I would prophesy every now and then, too. I had a spirit who had overtaken my body and I would cry on the altar during all-night prayer shut-ins, "Lord, deliver me!" Literally crying and begging God to please take this away from me. Anything that you can't live without is an addiction. We all have had or had issues and sin that we committed, however, I have decided to be honest about mine and my total deliverance. I'm not saying how many men I have slept with, but I will tell you that they were not my husband and therefore, that's what we call in Christendom, fornication. My struggle and issue was that of addiction to sex! Let's define addiction, *Addiction-a psychological and physical inability to stop consuming a chemical, drug, activity, or substance, even though it is causing psychological and physical harm.* Ok, so it's an activity that was causing me not only physical harm, but spiritual harm as well.

I began to find myself sleeping with men not for money, although I drove some of the biggest drug dealers in my county around and yes, I was sleeping with one of them. I was getting money, but because I was the driver. Oh, sin will take you further than you want to go and keep you longer than you ever want to stay. From the age of sixteen to twenty-one, I was completely out of control. Why was Latisha out of control? Because I never dealt with my issue and the pain that caused it. Rejection from not feeling wanted by my father, molested, raped and cheated on by men. I felt like no one loved me at one point in my life, not even my mother. I tried to take pills, cut my wrists, but by the grace of God, I'm still here to write my story for the world to read. I was seeking for someone to fill the deep void that was inside of my heart, along with it being broken most of my life. Trusting people, looking for a mother and father at times. My mother as I said did the best that she could, however, she worked three jobs and at times I would get fussed at, because I would take to some of the people at the church and I would take them as a mother figure, but more of a spiritual mother most times. I would always hear their names and endure verbal abuse. Just because I always was in church and with my church family, I was closer to them than my immediate family.

Jesus never cared too much about His actual immediate family, the Holy Writ declares in Matthew

12:46-50, "While he yet talked to the people, behold, his mother and his brethren stood without, desiring to speak with him. Then one said unto him, Behold, thy mother and thy brethren stand without, desiring to speak with thee. But he answered and said unto him that told him, who is my mother? And who are my brethren? And he stretched forth his hand toward his disciples, and said, Behold my mother and my brethren! For whosoever shall do the will of my Father which is in heaven, the same is my brother, and sister, and mother."

See, even Jesus wasn't close to His family. He said, those who do the will of His Father are His family. I'm not saying that my mother or my family wasn't doing the will of the Father, however, I was attending another ministry, different from my mother's, since the age of eleven. So, I became closer to my church family, who I saw far more often than my mother or brother. My mother would say I was disrespectful, because I wanted to go and be with my church family more than I wanted to be around the house. I stayed locked in my room when I was home and hardly came out, only when no one was home, or to eat and use the bathroom. I had never been normal as my mother would say, I never slept well and she would say when she was mad at me, that I should have been aborted when I was in her womb. However, I know that those words came from a place of pain. Pain of loving a man, who never will you marry, but you gave your all to him, thinking he was the man for you. Wow, how the cycle continues with me! However, my mother and I never had a great relationship as some mothers and daughters have had. Actually, my mother and I didn't become close until I turned about twenty-eight years old. Yes, she has been there through every sickness and surgery, like I said, she's done the best she could to be the best mother, but my mom was broken as well and raising two children on a fixed income wasn't easy. I would watch my mom write out the bills on an envelope every time she would get paid, budgeting her money and seeing what she had to pay. Never have my brother and I wanted for anything materialistic, I just lacked feeling love, due to the many hurtful and painful situations that occurred from my early childhood and would follow me throughout my adulthood; all of this played a major role in my life.

Yes, I was rebellious and I would leave and lie to go stay out sometimes. I was not where I said, but most times I was instead with a guy I was involved with trying to feel special. Sometimes even while going to church or amongst a crowd of people, I would always feel alone and like I was the only one in the room. Sex and men were my outlet to try to soothe some of the pain. I know Jesus is the answer for everything, but first you must allow Him to be everything for you and dwell within you, and I didn't want God fully in my life at that time. Later, I would learn that filling yourself with what feels good to fill voids or to try to heal your own brokenness, is only a temporary high or fix, and fades away quickly once the motion of the notion is gone, or you get that piece of pleasure for your fleshly desire and it's finished its course for that moment. It's like a drug addiction, once you get that hit for a few minutes you're on cloud nine, but when it's over, you feel more jacked up, messed up, empty and broken than before! Only God can fill voids and be everything to a person, and you will never get tired of Him or feel empty, but full. You won't feel horrible afterwards, but you will feel alive and fresh. When God comes into your life, a new life begins and you become not only more joyful and full, but free! I had to thirst after righteousness in order to be fulfilled by God. Matthew 5:6 says, "Blessed are they which do hunger and thirst after righteousness: for they shall be filled." I had to change my appetite towards the things of the Father, but it took a made up mind and a change of heart.

In my teenage years leading to my early adulthood years, I did anything to try to suppress the pain, while feeling depressed. I had fallen into a great depression. I had no self-love and I knew nothing about what's love got to do with it! Not knowing that only the Father's love mattered; that His love is everlasting and satisfying. To be satisfied means to be full, nothing else can fit, no room, no vacancy, occupied. I had to become full up with God and nothing else in the world or my sinful past, could fit anywhere in my space. My spiritual house had to become vacant and rearranged, in order for it to become occupied with what God was trying to give me. We must be able to give an eviction notice to the things that keep us in bondage and chained down in captivity; that includes anything that causes us to be weighted down and makes it hard to get up. But the Father is the Greatest Power in the universe, and He can fill your life with such a joy and you will be able to smile authentically and be able to live a great life on earth. There is no sin or issue from which the Father can't free you. All you have to do is confess your sin. In Romans 10: 9-10 you can find how to begin your new life. These two verses state, "That if you confess with your mouth the Lord Jesus and believe in your heart that God has raised Him from the dead, you will be saved. For with the heart one believes unto righteousness, and with the mouth confession is made unto salvation."

Now know that it is a day to day journey and change begins with you, with the Father guiding and helping you every day. There's a process in this Christian Faith Walk. It takes faith to keep walking into your newfound life. Although you may not see all that you may desire sometimes, you must have faith to stay on the right path to Heaven. *What is Faith- Now faith is the substance of things hoped for, the evidence of things not seen.* Hebrews 11:1. I may not see God, but I believe in my heart, that Jesus died for my sins and one day I'm going to live with Him in Heaven, I shall inherit my mansion and live with Him forever. Every day may not be easy, and tests and trials in Christendom will occur, but we must not give up or become disheartened. John 14:1-3 "Let not your heart be troubled: ye believe in God, believe also in me. In my Father's house are many mansions: if it were not so, I would have told you. I go to prepare a place for you. And if I go and prepare a place for you, I will come again, and receive you unto myself; that where I am, there ye may be also." Jesus died for our sins, and salvation is free, but there is a price to obtain the freedom that salvation freely gives. You must continue to choose what's right, even if wrong is present. Sometimes, choosing to do what is right is hard, but the reward is far greater than you or I could ever imagine. Stay encouraged and keep pressing forward.

4

The Me That's Been Overtaken By THEM

"Wherefore come out from among them, and be ye separate, saith the Lord, and touch not the unclean thing; and I will receive you. And will be a Father unto you, and ye shall be my sons and daughters, saith the Lord Almighty."

2 Corinthians 6:17

We all want to or we all should have the urge to want to be a better person throughout our lives. When we get into any type of relationship, no matter if it's friendship, romantic, brother, sister, spiritual or even natural; it should make us better or want to do better. Those who we allow to take up precedence in our life should enhance and also bring out the best in us, as we should as well for them. Sometimes, however, instead of doing so, because of voids and just wanting to be accepted, we embrace certain behaviors, some that are so corrupt, discrediting, foul and very disrespectful, to overshadow our lives. We begin living under the dark shadows of something or someone that are literally a death sentence to our lives! We must realize some relationship don't enhance us, but it really causes decomposition. Some relationships cause rotting to transpire inside of you. Killing you softly while your biological clock is ticking away and eventually you will explode or become exposed as trying to be someone that you are not, hiding in the shadows behind a mask that is worn throughout your life's journey and those around you really don't know the authentic you that is locked away, waiting to truly be revealed to the world. I found myself giving people the me that wasn't me, becoming what they wanted me to be and being who they wanted me to be. Honestly not loving me, but loving those who I allowed to intrude my space, life and time, to give them more than I will ever receive. I had a mindset that the more I would give and the more I buy, then they will see how much I cared for and loved them. I'll do whatever to keep those I carried in my heart close to me, even if they would mishandle me and cause me much pain. In all honesty, all I ever wanted was love and someone to love me as much if not more than I loved them. At times it seemed like the more they hurt me and degraded me, the more things I found myself doing for them. Latisha just like everyone else wanted to be loved, wanted and needed! I wanted these three things more than anything. I would do whatever to have just a measure of love, acceptance and wanting to be needed in someone's life. I lost my identity to those I allowed into my life and loved dearly. I lost Latisha, I lost my voice, my opinion, and my mind. The only thing I always really kept was my heart of forgiveness, and a heart that loved them unconditionally. I can honestly say that most of them I allowed to hold my heart, have it, or allowed them in my heart, have taken much advantage of my heart. I even noticed them laughing at me and my expression. Some would mishandle me just to see if I would still do things for them and love them. Some saw me and knew I would give my last, just to make sure they were good, but they never cared if I was good. It was like my tears and suffering were a wonderful, joyful addition to their lives. Every last one of them that had my heart or was a part of my heart, I loved them more than myself. I was willing to die for them if need be. I've always said, "I hate my heart and how I love so freely."

I have given until it hurts! I've given until I couldn't give anymore! Whatever they wanted I tried to give my best. I'm not perfect and I never said I was. I am very certain that those I allowed into my life and I in theirs, I didn't cross every "T" and dot every "I" with them. Please also know that I'm not just talking about a relationship with me and a man, but also those I took as mothers, sisters, brothers and friends as well. I would love these individuals so hard and so much that when they mistreated me, I wouldn't know how to respond or just let it or they go. I would beg for them to stay in my life, pleading, "please don't leave me" or I would, "plead please, what do I have to do for you not to leave." It didn't even matter if they were toxic for me and meant no good. I could care less about their past or present and how it would affect me later on in life, even if I may hurt, cry, and be left for dead later on, with my arms stretched out, saying "help me," but it was like I literally was in the world by myself at times.

I had very difficult decisions to make at times, especially, should I stay or go? Thinking I could change some of them and their ways. I would further think, *perhaps if I continue to stay and cover them, they will eventually see my loyalty and love me no matter what.* I would always say, "I'm not going anywhere and I love you unconditionally." I'm here to report that all of what I did or say didn't work, it only cost me to pick up the broken and shattered pieces of my heart. I had to learn how to save and love Latisha!

You can't make anyone stay or love you. You must love yourself more than anything. You can't change folks; they have to want it. As my Second Mother, Apostle Dr. T.L. Penny would say to me as she would stay on the phone with me for hours when I needed guidance and help, "Latisha, you can't change them, they're not going to change and the only thing you will change is their diaper when they get old!" You can pray to God all you want, but until that person wants to change for real, they will never change.

You can't make anyone love you, be with you or see your true worth, it's all voluntary. While trying to change them, you will suffer inwardly and eventually it will affect your appearance outwardly. They must want to, and then act it out. It's just like a physically abusive relationship that for a few days they are so sweet and loving, and then out of nowhere they become so rude and very ugly. They keep you around, because they know you love them or they keep you around for a cover-up so that the Masquerade they are wearing will continue to conceal their true face of lies and their real identity of being someone else behind closed doors. Oftentimes in public they are the perfect couple or relationship, but in private they are dogging each other out to others and after a while will dog them out in front of their face. Before long, the façade of their acting caring quickly fades away. They begin to hide their phone, exchanging text messages at all times of night, and lying about where they are going and why. You confront them and they always make you feel crazy and then, because they seem like the perfect person to the public and in their eyes, you are made to look like you are the bad person. It's always you at fault, never them.

Yet, even with evidence of the truth and their hidden agendas and their double lives, you choose to stay, because you feel like perhaps one day they will see who you are and they will change. Making decisions of through sickness or health, even when not being married yet. Me loving them more than myself. Whether man or woman, we must set boundaries and have standards. If a person you are dating doesn't give more than you do, or at least try to give more than you do, you must know your worth and accept the fact that he or she is not the one for you. Never play a role for which you haven't gone through the proper proceedings, which placed you in that role. I was willing to give up my health and possibly die, leaving my family, just to be with them. These people didn't truly love me, nor were they in love with me. They were keeping secrets and covering things up, all the while never even trying to look out for me. Never fighting for me, or for us. I was allowing mistreatment from those who whom I held in high regards. They made it seem like I was troubled and crazy, while hiding all of their lies and secret battles. There were others in our relationships, other men and women. It seemed everyone was being loved, but myself.

I didn't care, I guess I was so wanting to be loved and

accepted that I would do just about anything, and I lowered my standards for people who didn't value my worth and what I had to offer. However, I can't blame them alone, because I didn't value myself either. I didn't have self-love, and no one can mishandle you or treat you unfairly unless you allow them to do so. I gave my power away to people and then, because I lost my power they were able to control me and place me in a robotic state to manipulate me and their wish was my command. I only wanted to please them and I became locked in a prison of my own making. I had to want to be free from them and love myself to the point that I saw that I was priceless, because of the price that Jesus paid for me to be free, when He died on Calvary's Cross. People, we must love ourselves more than anything or anyone else in this entire world. We must give God the infinite us. We must give Him our all without any second thought or reservation. I had placed trust and power in men and women. Now I had to take that trust and power back and obtain the power I was given, which comes with the gift of the Holy Ghost, and I had to learn to trust God wholeheartedly.

5

When You Love Them… More Than

"I am the Lord thy God, which have brought thee out of the land of Egypt, out of the house of bondage. Thou shalt have no other gods before me." **Exodus 20:1-3**

I was looking for validation, acceptance and love from whomever, and however I could get it. That included those I took as a mother figure, which was mainly spiritual more than anything else. However, when it came to the men, I was looking for that one true love who would be faithful and true, but I always ended up with the wrong man or allowed the wrong person into my personal space. Looking for love in all the wrong places instead of accepting the Father's unconditional love that He always was waiting for me to see and receive. When you are broken and you have given up on yourself, you will settle for anything that appears to look good and looks like love. Chasing behind people, trying to always fix what was wrong and begging them to stay and not leave me. Afraid of being rejected and unloved. Hiding behind the mask of what they all wanted me to be, and what they wanted me to do, but not being who God has chosen me to be and what He wanted me to do.

Every relationship no matter what kind, I became disfigured and I began losing pieces of me by being in these unhealthy toxic relationships. Acceptance is all I wanted, but most of them didn't care about the pieces of Latisha, and Latisha didn't care at all either. The way I would show my love to people was always with gifts of any kind and giving monetary gifts. That was my way of saying I love you! So many have taken for granted those kinds of nice gestures and many acts of kindness. I never was buying love, that's just the way I was. Mind you, I'm giving of myself, and forgiving them, even after some had lied, cheated, talked about me, laughed at my struggles, and embarrassed me, and for some ironic reason they all thought I would never get tired of any of it. I was married to a man that had many issues, but hiding behind the church so they couldn't see his flaws at all. Not marrying him once, but twice. He left almost every six months no lie and had everyone thinking that it was me. I was more single than married. I always forgave him for all and never held what he did against him.

I really just wanted my family. My aunt and spiritual mother, Pastor Avis Frasier, taught me how to take care of a husband. My biological mother didn't get married until I was twenty-four years old. Pastor Frasier is an excellent wife and an example of how to care for your high priest and home. She would make me bring the plate to any guest that her husband, my uncle, Apostle Frasier would bring home. I often stayed in their home. Their home was my second home growing up. Pastor Frasier gave me the tools I needed to be a good, Godly wife. Aunt Avis instilled in me Godly principles and how to be a holy example. When I think of a Lady in the Kingdom of God, she is the first person that comes to mind. A Real Pastor's Wife.

However, no matter what she may have taught me, when it came to being a good, Godly wife, it didn't matter to my ex-husband, while we were married. I would cook every day and bring his plate to him, drive him to work, because he didn't have a license, wash and iron his clothes and took him back every time he would come back. I was taking mental and physical abuse until my self-esteem was so low that I would post inspiration notes to myself all over my house, especially looking in the mirror, to tell myself that I am beautiful and I am important. I ended up taking him back a total of four times, while he'd gone away doing whatever he wanted and I stayed at home praying and remaining faithful, asking God to please send my husband back to me.

My Christian roots played a major part of why I didn't divorce him. I believe in what I was taught by the Apostolic Faith, you wait until your husband comes back and remain faithful. In 2008, I had got in five-car collision while pregnant with our daughter and I couldn't get a check until after I gave birth to her. So, in 2009, a week before me having back surgery, he left and said, "Let your mom take care of you." He has never been in our daughter's life for even six months since she was born, and she is ten years old now. I really was struggling to understand what was taking place, because by this time I had stopped playing church and I was sold out to God, before I would meet Him years later. So, my question to the Father was, what did I do wrong? However, the last time my husband left was in November 2010 with a Dear Latisha letter, after I was in church and he was pretending he was at work, kissing me that morning and saying he loved me. Taking the truck I bought and leaving me in it. Taking my new Expedition truck and putting it in a title loan and me having to go into my children's trust fund to pay for it. Having won six figures in 2010, because of the accident in 2008 and then having to spend it and losing it through helping people and being with the wrong man. Giving myself to men who had caused me to lose so much, but I allowed it! I went from having six figures in the bank in 2010, to not having but $10,000 left once he would leave. He was stealing money from me and trying to literally steal my state of mind and self-esteem.

I finally got a divorce and was getting healed properly, but not long afterwards I became involved with another man and then another, that wasn't designed for me and I wasn't a fit for him... This has always been the story of Latisha Loving Them More Than... Willing to lose and never winning. Willing to die or to live in a life filled with misery. Dating guys who didn't know my worth and would hurt me in the worst way, taking a part of me with them every time. I kept asking, *what have I done wrong? Why can't you just love me?* I was willing to sacrifice much, gaining so little from them. Covering them as they lived a double life. I was willing to sacrifice all just to have them in my life, blinded by my love, not theirs. Never telling their secrets, but saying I'll take it to my grave, while they got people looking at me funny and themselves looking like a saint. These men I can honestly say were just as I was, broken, and there was a root that grew into a strong tree, these men also had a root as well that was never dealt with and they lacked healing for themselves. How could they love me fully with their heart when they were so broken themselves?

On many occasions I tried to end my life, but God blocked it each time. All my life I've fought for my life. I've always felt like I've been in a ring never having a break to breathe or to smile. May I be totally honest? As time passed, I gave up on smiling and being happy, because I've had so many disappointments in my life. If I would smile it was a fake one that covered the Broken Latisha, who never could maintain a full grip on her life and come to full terms with life's hang-ups and what it's all about. We sing a song in Christendom, "That trouble don't last always..." well, I was trying to figure out when my trouble will end. Loving the wrong man caused me to almost lose 8 1/2 years of my life in prison, but I ended up only doing 247 days. Loving the wrong man caused me to sacrifice my inner peace and peace of mind. Loving the wrong man caused me to settle for less than I was worth. Loving the wrong man had caused me to put my own health in jeopardy, because my heart was too far into it! Loving the wrong man more than me, caused me to make poor choices when it came to my well-being and perhaps suffering more than the Father ever intended me to. Loving the wrong man would cause me to get pregnant out of wedlock and have a son, who is a perfect gift from God that I don't at all regret having. Loving the wrong man would cause me to become engaged to a deacon in the church and getting pregnant with twins and he would ask me to abort them, just so his cover wouldn't be blown. I did it, but I still didn't end up being his wife after putting my body through that. Me loving the wrong man would cause me to marry the wrong man and get pregnant with twins, losing one and not knowing that the other was in my tubes and having to go and receive a shot to terminate the pregnancy. Then my ex-husband would leave me for the first time thereafter. Loving the wrong man caused me to be physically, mentally, verbally, and emotionally abused and to fall into a great depression. My heart, mind, body and soul were so into these relationships with these men; it's really unbelievable the things I was willing to sacrifice. We must remember that God is a jealous God and I was placing people, mainly men in the place where He should have been alone. I was looking to receive from them what only God can give to me.

Wrestling with a person who apparently doesn't want you for the same reason why you wanted and married them, is tragic. I was losing my self-worth and practically losing my mind fighting for something that takes both parties, not just one. I also lost seven years of running behind a man who didn't want me and would lie to folks claiming that it's just me, because he's quiet in the world and a hellion in the closed four walls of the home.

It took years of healing and years to recover some of the missing parts of me. I gave up on me, but I'm very grateful that God didn't give up on me, but He kept me on His mind and Jesus sat at the right hand of the Father making intercession for me while I was a wretch undone. Surely, I'm glad that I'm alive to write this book, because if it wasn't for the grace of God I would have been dead a long time ago and God had every right to have taken my life, because of my wicked and sinful ways. Listen, I should have had some type of STD or disease that I couldn't be healed or cured from, but thank you Daddy God, you never allowed that to come upon me, even with knowledge of some things and me putting my life in harm's way. However, I'm here writing and reporting victory and that the verdict is that I have been set free from all sadness and guilt, thinking that I had to be something to and for people, who would never be what I was for them. God freed me and healed me from the inside out!

6

GRABBING THE PIECES OF ME

"But the God of all grace, who hath called us unto his eternal glory by Christ Jesus, after that ye have suffered a while, make you perfect, stablish, strengthen, settle you." **1 Peter 5:10**

I was looking for unconditional love that will stick and stay with me no matter what, but God is the only one who is capable of doing that. I was very distorted in thinking I could give my heart to anyone and they will never mishandle it and they would be able to take care of it. I put all my trust in them and I shouldn't, but I did. They broke my heart, even those

I became closest to that weren't male figures. Not even my mother or father had the tools to piece my broken heart together, because the heartbreak started with them. They were a part of my disappointments and they didn't handle me with care. I had to be repaired by the potter Himself and allow Him to remake and remold me all over again, into a great purified masterpiece fit and ready for the use of the Father. I had to allow God to grab the pieces of Latisha that were all over the world and freely given by Latisha.

It was time for a great change, which would last and not be just a temporary fix. Sometimes we want things to change, but change must begin within us. I had to want to change and become better. Change is good and anything that doesn't want to change, becomes a misfit and will be in a chaotic state. Change is a sign of growth. I actually lost me totally and I thought there was no hope for me anymore. At one point in my life I had become so lost and in a state of bewilderment. I remember calling my second mother who was my confidante and saying, "Mommy, I feel like I'm in a dark place" and she replied, "You are coming out and up out of the dark place." That next month of her speaking that into my life, a hurtful, but necessary breakthrough had occurred. I had gotten to such a place that I felt low and worthless. I had gotten myself involved an a very façade-type relationship and I tried everything to try to love this guy and to make him see that I loved him, but no matter what I would do, it was never enough. I felt lost and trapped and I experienced a sense of guilt that I had to stay. I cried every day being in this relationship and no one knew the massive abuse with which I was having to deal. I was made to feel as though I must stay and be there and I wanted to, because I loved him unconditionally with my whole heart and I was willing to die for this guy. Please note, however, that he didn't truly want me or for me to stay, because he would tell others that he didn't want me around, all the while telling me that he did. However, this young man loved others far more than me.

I thought maybe if I do whatever for him, and buy him whatever, then perhaps it would turn his heart towards me, but in time I realized that there was never going to be a change. However, I stayed anyways and I didn't care for the evidence of things I saw with my own eyes, the many encounters with those who he was cheating on me with, but I covered for him. Even though he never appreciated my loyalty, I remained loyal. He would shun me around certain people and I remember one time, I asked questions and he clapped in my face and got up from the table and left me at the restaurant. Every time I would ask questions regarding what I knew and saw that was very true, he would get so angry at me. But it wasn't me, it was a spiritual war going on behind the scenes. I believe I was in his life for him to have a second chance and I was a part of his deliverance, but he didn't want any of that. He would ignore my calls and go missing, but me not loving myself enough, I would stay until whenever he returned. I loved this guy more than anyone in my life or even my own life. I had a very hard decision to make: should I stay or go? I stayed. It eventually took much counsel, prayer, and fasting for me to be set free.

In order for me to get delivered and grab the pieces of me, I had to erase pictures, throw away gifts, erase emails, and anything that would remind me of him. I really thought that I needed to stay. I was playing savior, which had consistently hurt me badly, because there's only one who can save. I almost married a murderer, believe me or not, but the assassination attempt was an absolute fail. I'm so grateful to God for the healing and restoration that took place. It took years, but I was set free. I'm forever grateful for my second Mother, Apostle Dr. T.L. Penny for loving me and helping to nurture me back to health, through the word, talks and just being there through so much that I couldn't even share without uncovering some hard truths about the individual. However, I thank God for total deliverance and realizing that I am worth more than just being there and not being loved, by people only tolerating me, and using me when they had need of me. I thereafter begin to Love Latisha again and seeing what I am worth again. Piece by Piece, I'm regaining the authentic Latisha back. I thank God for saving my life, when I had made a decision of shortening my life.

7

ME VS ME

"Simon, Simon, Satan has asked to sift all of you as wheat. But I have prayed for you, Simon, that your faith may not fail." **Luke 22:31**

O rder, Order, Order in Latisha's life! The chaos and malfunction of my life must come to a halt and line up with what the Father thinks of me, what He called me, what He has ordained me to be and chosen me to be from the foundation of the world. Being confident of this very thing, that he which hath begun a good work in

Latisha will perform it until the day of Jesus Christ: Philippians 1:6.

What God has started, He is God enough to finish it. Latisha is everywhere and nowhere to be found. Lost in people, through ministry, lost in helping everyone else, but herself. I always believed in being and giving the best I can and doing for all I allow in my heart. My motto, "I'm not responsible for how people treat me, but I'm responsible for how I treat people." When my ex-husband walked out for the first time after being married for only six months in 2004, the Father said to me, "I'm teaching you how to walk in forgiveness!" Yes, just like God, He would teach me one of the greatest lessons through my heartache and pain. However, I trusted Him when I could trace Him! Job said, "Though he slay me, yet will I trust in him: but I will maintain mine own ways before him." Job 13:15.

I didn't understand why would God wanted to teach me this lesson during this fragile time in my life. I wanted to be petty and I wanted to hide from the shame of being a part of a failed marriage. However, I had to face the hard truth that you must forgive those who have wronged you, even while still feeling the pain. Forgiveness is never easy and I wanted to remain mad with everyone who had ever done me wrong, but I couldn't and move forward with life. If you don't forgive, it will eventually affect you and you will become bitter and forgiveness will eat at you like cancer if you don't forgive. So, first, I had to forgive my father for not being there for me when I was growing up and how I saw that he took care of other children, instead of me being a girl and not only that, the baby girl. I had to forgive him for rejecting me. Then I had to forgive both of my parents together, who I felt dropped me when I was younger and didn't pay attention to me being troubled at the age of five when my private body parts were being mishandled and messed over, and then the cycle continued until the age of thirteen. I never felt safe or worthy of someone ever wanting me. I felt as though I was dropped and my legs were broken and I never would or could recover at one time, but thank God for my healing. I had to forgive my mother for the very mean and hateful things that she would say out of her mouth, and the names she would call me when I would want to be around my church family. I had to forgive her for calling me fat and ugly or her calling me a name one day followed by her saying, "I hope you crash into a tree and wrap around it and die." She would also say that I was disrespectful and that I acted like this one or that one.

I was always the child who worked and tried to help when I could, but it was never enough. I never recall hearing her say she was proud of me, but instead she'd say that she hated me when she got angry and would even say that she wished I was never born. Sometimes she would take it even further, blaming me for the things that happened to me during my childhood. I had to also forgive every man that I felt as though had hurt me and used me. I had to forgive them, because it wasn't totally their fault, it was mine as well. I had to forgive those who molested me, and be able to face them without any malice in my heart. I needed to forgive the two men who raped me. I had to forgive all the women who I took and placed in my heart, trying to make them mother me, but I got upset when they couldn't, because it wasn't their assignment to do so. I had to forgive the pastors that mishandled me and told me I wouldn't ever be anything. I had to forgive the pastors whose leadership I was under, but instead of them loving and guiding me with their staff they poked me and cut me with the end of the hook and caused me to bleed out. I had to forgive all those who broke my heart while loving them and they didn't love me back. I had to forgive those who lied about me to others to make themselves look grand. I had to forgive those who used me and borrowed money and never paid me back. I had to forgive the fathers of my two children, for leaving me to raise my son and daughter by myself and not giving me the help I needed, when I needed it. I had to forgive every man that proposed to me and we didn't get married, because of one reason or the other. I had to repent to God, because for a minute I became angry with Him and I rebelled at times. I had to ask for Him to forgive me for acting out and trying to end my life which is filled with so much purpose. Most importantly, I had to forgive me, Latisha. I had to forgive myself and all the many times I messed up and I showed out. I had to forgive myself for all the times I allowed men to have their way with me, and not loving myself enough to not let that happen.

I also had to accept the fact that I was trying to fight the enemy or the one we call Satan, but I was the enemy to myself all that time. I was the only one who could help me, but only with a repentant and a forgiving heart. I had to have a total makeover and I had to accept what I didn't want to accept, that I really didn't love myself and who God had chosen me to be. I was mad with me, not them. I was living a double life and I needed to change my life habits that only were leading to a permanent destruction, and leading me to death and on my way to hell.

In order for deliverance to take place you must recognize that you have a major problem and you need help. You can't do it on your own and you can't continue to do the same thing and expect different results. One must be willing to accept all the charges that are set before them. One must be willing to look in the mirror and admit that they are their biggest impediment to becoming great and living their best life with Christ. One must be willing to give up the old and put on the new.

8

FACING THE HARD FACTS

"If my people, which are called by my name, shall humble themselves, and pray, and seek my face, and turn from their wicked ways; then will I hear from heaven, and will forgive their sin, and will heal their land." **2 Chronicles 7:14**

Cutting away the corruption of the old to put on and wear the new. In order to face the facts you must first deal with the lies that you created to make yourself and others feel secure about who you are. There must be a peeling away of the facade that you have made up to become something or someone that you're not. What is a lie? A lie is an assertion that is believed to be false, typically used with the purpose of deceiving someone.

Now what is a fact? A fact is a thing that is a known or proved to be true.

We must remove the built-up corrosion of the past that has been covered by makeup throughout the years and deal with self, not the artificial, but the real authentic self. The Authentic One, that cries when the mask is taken off at home in the bedroom. The authentic one, which at times thought about ending it all. The authentic self that feels like fighting and beating up and hurting those who have hurt you in the past. The real you that didn't want church, but wanted to stay home and chill. The real you that is sick of the pastors and their crying and talking about sheep bites, snake bites, etc... And you want to say, "where were you when I needed you? Why are you always using your rod to stab us and poke us and wound us, when you are supposed to use the rod with care for correction and not abuse?" Sick of the church and what it has become and has changed its stand for dancing, who pays the most, clicks, chicks, and gents. Tired of living holy while others are living a shabby life and you giving your all, your gifts, money and time and your all isn't good enough at all. Yes, we do it unto the Lord, but just as the shepherds want to feel appreciated, so do the sheep... can we get some love, too! Can we get a "thanks" instead of, "well, that's what you all are supposed to do" or have to do. Sick sick sick of myself in the church and having to keep quiet instead of revealing who I am, because I'm afraid of the judgement or the whisper that will occur later. Hearing God speak in my ear, but I can't say it, because either the ones in leadership don't believe in your gift and the anointing on your life, or I'm not their so-called favorite and therefore, I won't say anything. Sometimes it's a word of warning for the church at large, but you're afraid that the leader will rebuke you, because they don't want the sin revealed! Tired of just sitting and wasting away. Helping everyone and neglecting myself and what I need and want. The fact of it all is that most of us want to be accepted by people who have their own ways, who live one way in church and in the light of the world, but are a totally different person at home or at work and remain in darkness which has a very dimmed light.

All of us have issues that if it wasn't for the blood of Jesus that washes and covers, we all would have been exposed. However, some of us fight our fleshly desires and take very seriously this walk in Christ. I begin to negate the pieces of me, so that I can fit in. Shutting my mouth so I can be liked and loved. Holding to the words of those who said I would never be anything and I couldn't do this and that, which suppressed my true talents and gifts! The suppressing of my opponents caused me to fall into a great depression for over twenty-two years of my life and I'm only thirty-eight years old now. No one really knew, because I wore a mask and would cry in the dark hidden away. Please never be afraid of getting help if you need it. Some things you can try to pray away, but some things we need to let out by talking. You're not crazy by getting help, you're crazy if you don't.

I never wanted to hurt people, however, I always wanted to get rid of me. Depression is real and this is why people should be careful how they handle others and what they may say. I didn't know how badly I suffered from depression until I fell so deeply into it, and I would want to drive far away and drive over a bridge, or the time I was at the beach and I thought about just walking into the middle of the ocean and drowning myself. It became a time when I wanted to slit my throat with a butcher knife, because I was so tired of my heart being broken in life or the time when I was sitting in my car and contemplating ending it and my son came and got me out of the car and carried my things into the house while my shirt was soaked with tears in April of 2018.

The last encounter with depression and wanting to commit suicide was in November 2018, when I was working a security site and I was so down, I felt like my children would have been better off without me. I felt like I had failed them as being a mother. Not being able to pay my bills and stay afloat. After having four evictions and moving five times and not being able to find a decent job. Feeling alone and abandoned by people to whom you have given your heart. Always giving, always doing and getting nothing in return, barely crumbs. Dealing with folks who know your struggle, but would rather laugh and talk about you than help and uplift you. Trusting and being deceived by the ones you trust. Settling and not choosing me and my happiness and even my health. Failed relationships and being lied to countless times. Evidence of the one you were madly in love with lying and cheating on you for years. Which seems as it was my life story. I felt not good enough and worthless to be here on earth. Loving and sacrificing. I wanted to stop the beat of the heart that continued to be broken time and time again. So, in front of Big Lots on a rainy night, I took out my gun and just when I was about to pull the trigger I received a text which I knew was God, because this was one of the people who had caused much pain and damage as well. As I tried to love again and trust again, he was full of lies and deceit. From the beginning, I should have run, but didn't. However, God intercepted death with a text and immediately I dropped my gun and I began to yell, "God, you really love me!" I felt like I had just been beaten, I never ever before had gone through such a spiritually intense warfare where I almost actually did it. I felt so drained.

Oftentimes in my life I felt imprisoned the most. I felt trapped like my life was just running its course with me merely being a shell, with nothing but existing, not really living at all. Very unhappy, walking halfway dead and lost. I had finally lost me and my smile. From the year of 2014 through the latter part of 2018, I double masked and I was covering my wounds and bleeding so much, until it would soon ooze out and everyone would see it. I was tired of being hit in the same spot of my heart. I literally got tired and began to peel of the layers of deceitful ways that I had clothed myself in, so no one would see my open wounds or even my scars. I was in a prison and I had to decide to get delivered from the spirit of depression and send the enemy back, with the oppression as well. The only way I could get delivered, though, was by accepting the fact that I can't make everyone happy and I can't please everyone either. I can't be everything to everyone. I'm not a savior, I need the Savior. I finally had a real "come to me, Jesus" moment and I had to do what makes Latisha happy. Even if I was barely walking, I'd crawl to press for my deliverance from people, which would bring a mighty deliverance for me. I had to save Latisha, she's worth saving and keeping alive. I came to a vital decision to choose me and my children. So, I prayed and made some healthy life-changing decisions for my life. I wanted to be free of the opinions of others and I wanted my freedom and my joy back. I allowed my joy to be taken from me by making others little gods in my life. Doing everything they wanted and I was like a yes woman to those I really wanted in my life. I had to learn to expect nothing from people, and if they do for me, then to simply appreciate them and say thank you and move on. You can be free from whatever or whomever you've allowed to bind you.

It doesn't matter how much you feel imprisoned, you can be set free through the blood and purification of Jesus Christ Our Lord. He is the only one that is able to give you a complete clean slate and there will be no more memories of your past behind the bars that others or you might have placed in front of you. Be Free, Be Delivered and Be Healed!

9

REFORM
TO CONFORM

"And be not conformed to this world: but be ye transformed by the renewing of your mind, that ye may prove what is that good, and acceptable, and perfect, will of God." **Romans 12:2**

One must get tired of their current situation and ways. I myself had to get sick and tired of me. I had to want to change and want all deliverance to take place. For me, it took multiple deliverances to take place. Why? Because I had done so much and put myself through so much! I had to go before the Lord and constantly lay out before Him. I also had to run from what I got delivered from, which was men and how they made me feel good. Many times, especially for women, we don't realize that when we lay down with a man that a part of their spirit enters into us. So, I had to go through a process of divorcement from each man that I had slept with, because those men weren't my husband. When that man penetrates you, it's an entry of invite. To penetrate means-*go into or through (something), especially with force or effort, gain access to.* There is a force that has taken over your body, and one that is mighty and full of a personality that isn't yours. So, you have to get rid of those who you allowed inside of you. It didn't happen until I wanted change. I was in the church, but the church wasn't in me. See, you can dress up the outside and look like you are well put together, but your inside is without question, jacked-up and messed up. It's imperative that your outside matches your inside. If not, you are perpetuating a fraud. You must be willing to change everything about you, but you can't fix yourself, you must allow the Father to fix you. You must be willing to switch teams and garments. New garments that will help you, and stand the test of time when the enemy comes to try and test you. I had to make a cautious decision of change.

I had to change my mindset and turn my heart and life to the Father for healing and restoration. I had to want to live a holy and a consecrated life before Him. How did I do this? I had to put on the Whole Armor of God. Ephesians 6:11-13 says, "Put on the whole armour of God, that ye may be able to stand against the wiles of the devil. For we wrestle not against flesh and blood, but against principalities, against powers, against the rulers of the darkness of this world, against spiritual wickedness in high places. Wherefore take unto you the whole armour of God that ye may be able to withstand in the evil day, and having done all, to stand."

To be fully armed we must have on our WAR-GARMENTS; ready and well-equipped with a survival kit, that will help us to stand when the adversary approaches. One must always be honest and true to one's self in order to receive true deliverance. Some may say that I don't have a problem or an issue, but if you can't help it or control it, it's a problem that's a huge issue. You must be real with yourself and who you have become. To be delivered means to- *be set free, to be cleansed from a spirit, meaning anything that has overtaken you.* Deliverance that causes you to be free from sin. Anything that causes you to act out, to do the opposite of what's righteous and holy as the Bible has commanded, is sinful and you need to be free from it. You are in bondage and you can't do it yourself, and you have to want to change your behavior. I had to become satisfied with Christ being the head of my life and also being in my life. To be satisfied means to be full and without lack. It wasn't until I became vacant in order to have the right occupancy. I remember in the spring of 2001 I was cleaning my room and doing some spring cleaning and God said, do some spiritual cleaning as well. At the time I still had things from my exes and I still had a residue of remembrance. So, I began to throw away everything that any of them ever gave me. That's when my true deliverance took place. I found myself throwing away items, pictures, erasing text messages, changing my number and anything that had something to do with them and me. Sometimes you can't hold on to anything, it's too much to keep; it's a reminder of them and what you all had and what you all had done. When you want deliverance, you will do anything to be free. You will let go of what you once welcomed and embraced, to grab and hold on to what's new and those greater things to come.

10

DAMAGED GOODS STILL HOLD GOODS

"But ye are a chosen generation, a royal priesthood, an holy nation, a peculiar people; that ye should shew forth the praises of him who hath called you out of darkness into his marvellous light; Which in time past were not a people, but are now the people of God: which had not obtained mercy, but now have obtained mercy." **1 Peter 2: 9-10**

One thing that is a known fact, is that a canned good can be thrown several times and the can will become very disfigured and out of its normal shape, but no matter what damage is on the outside, it's what is inside the can, that still holds the goods. What is inside of that can is still able to be seasoned and cooked to the cook's perfection. Man looks on the outer appearance, but our God looks upon and inside the heart of a man. It doesn't matter how your outside may look, but what does your heart say? We often try to compare ourselves and lives to others, but those whom we mark as having and living their best lives, in many cases really aren't living such a life at all. As a matter of fact, most of them are very unhappy, because it's not about what you can buy or even give at times, it's about first having Christ, which causes you to be rich, and no kind of sorrow comes along with it. Sometimes we compare our lives with others and what they may have, but we aren't thankful for what we ourselves are blessed to have. We that seemingly don't have that much, are actually full of rich treasures and we don't even know it.

I believe that it's not when or how you start, but finishing is the true goal of success. So many of us have focused on others in their success, until we lose sight of our own success and working towards our purpose in life. Some like myself have encountered major setbacks in life, that when we feel like we have taken 10 steps forward we are knocked down and backwards about 30 feet. However, please be encouraged that you haven't died, and as long as you have breath in your body there is great hope, to try again and go forth. You have endured and have overcame everything that has happened in your life thus far life. You're not a failure, you actually are a conqueror, because you could have given up, but you didn't. You actually lived to go on and walk forward towards your destiny. Many of my peers and colleagues in the gospel seem as though they have surpassed me and honestly most of them have, but there is always a turning point where the table turns, or may I say that the sun will shine on your side of the earth. There is a season for everything as the holy writ proclaims in Ecclesiastes 3.

I had to learn and appreciate the seasons of my life and when they changed. No season is the same, there's a season of winter, spring, summer, and fall and all four of them have a serving purpose. You must be willing to understand the season which you are in.

Seasons are forever changing and we should not worry about those who may seem like they are flourishing more than us, especially if they are not of the Faith. The Bible says, "Not to fret ourselves because of evildoers, neither be envious against the workers of iniquity." Psalms 37:1. I surely and painfully regret the offers that were fast and looked glamorous to me. See, the enemy will make everything look so right and good, but after a while in it, you become devastated and left empty and almost dead. We must realize that the enemy's job is to steal, kill, and destroy and however and whatever he has to do to accomplish his job, so that you will fail at your job, he will do so. The enemy will never dangle anything that you wouldn't want in your face. He knows what's appealing to you and what you like. However, we must always listen to the Father and the Holy Ghost which will guide us. He doesn't have to be loud, He can softly speak and it will be effective.

We must understand that the enemy comes to abort your spiritual baby and he doesn't want you to come forth and do the will of the Father. I'm here to encourage you that you shouldn't worry about people or even those who don't think that you qualify or are equipped; there are a set of people who are waiting on you and only you can help to free them from the bondage that has kept them weighted down and imprisoned. You can never judge a book by its cover Man looks on the outer appearance, but our God looks upon the heart of a man or woman. When it was time for Samuel to pick a king, he was looking at the outer appearance and how they looked very fit to his eyes, however the king was smelly, small in stature and doing a job that probably no one wanted, but God was preparing David for greatness. While tending to sheep, he was fighting tigers, lions and bears, he was in training the entire time to be able to rule a kingdom. The one that they counted out will be the one who is not afraid to go out and face a giant and kill him. Many may have counted you out, and to be honest we counted our own selves out as well, but we are chosen to accomplish a mighty work for the kingdom.

The trials that we have faced were preparing us for our destiny. It's not what has happened to you or even happening to you right now that defines your life story, it's how you will go through your obstacles, conquer them, and come out at the end. You must continue to press forward until the end. Never giving up, but stay the course and finish, no matter what the challenges may be. Don't throw in the towel, but use it to wipe your sweat as you run this race. Scripture states that the race is not given to the swift, nor the battle to the strong. Quitting is never an option, and I'm here to encourage you to keep going. You may be broken and need healing, but I promise you that God will heal you as you go forward. Sometimes the process of healing takes place as we work for His kingdom, helping others not to make the same mistakes as we did.

I can tell you that everything that happened had to happen, and it serves such a miraculous purpose that will help to free so many. The nations await the YOU that has been waiting to be revealed. Never be ashamed of the scars of your past shortcomings. Show your scars so that you can show how our great God has healed you. You hold the goods that will add life and flavor to someone's life. Your past doesn't define you, your present and future does. You are not him or her anymore, and you don't have to prove it, just live righteously and pull others up as you continue to walk forward with your head held high. Dust your brothers and sisters off and pick them up and go to the next and the next. Help save someone's life as Christ and others have helped you. This is why I decided to show my scars of my life and I pray that you know through this book, that you can make it and live life to the fullest.

11

NOW THAT THE MASQUERADE IS OVER

"And I will restore to you the years that the locust hath eaten, the cankerworm, and the caterpillar, and the palmerworm, my great army which I sent among you. And ye shall eat in plenty, and be satisfied, and praise the name of the Lord your God, that hath dealt wondrously with you: and my people shall never be ashamed." **Joel 2:24-5**

When you have a coming to Jesus moment, in a good way of course, everything becomes new and new life will begin. No more does one have to hide their true self to irreverent people. One thing that we must realize is that there's nothing we can do in our entire life that the Father doesn't know about or has allowed. Our lives are predestined before the foundation of this world. However, there is a blessed assurance that He who has begun a good work in you and me, He shall perform it. No matter how long it takes, God can make it seem like time stood still; just to make time for you to catch up. God shall redeem the time for you when you have made up your mind to let go of the facade past that you have made up for so many years. You and I have worn a Masquerade mask far too long! It had become our daily routine and no one knew who we really were until we left the Masquerade party of our lives that had literally been holding us back from our purpose and destiny. All of us were born with a great purpose that requires a mighty work. Everything that has happened or will happen in the future is all connected to our destined purpose. Even those hard obstacles that we faced, were put there or allowed to be there in order to make us stronger to pull someone out later on from what we have overcome and conquered.

Let me encourage you, you survived all of it. How can I say this declaration? Because you are reading this book, and this lets me know that what may have come to overtake or even assassinate you, didn't work. All of the hurt, shame, and the pain was for such a time as this. You cried, you wanted to end it all, you wanted to die, but now that you and I have come and faced our truth, we have now been delivered. You now are your real true self and you can help save others. Now the mask has been destroyed and we must be who God said and made us to be. He never saw you as a failure, He saw you as His chosen vessel. He loved you through the wrong and saw that you one day would become right. His love is greater than anything you've ever done. Nothing can change the way the Father feels about you! From now on, live and go forward knowing that the Father is with you and no one else can be you, like you. We must be careful not to change who we are, to become who others may want us to be. We must love the person we are and only change to become better for yourself, and want to be all that the Father has required us to be. Lose who you are for Him, never anyone else.

LATISHA R. MITCHELL

12

THE REVEAL

"He hath made every [thing] beautiful in his time: also he hath set the world in their heart, so that no man can find out the work that God maketh from the beginning to the end."
Ecclesiastes 3:11

Will the real you please arise and reveal yourself? It's hard to break old ancient habits, but it can be done. Some of us have been wearing a mask for others and being what they wanted us to be until we actually have become

81

accustomed to faking it until we make it. This must stop! No more faking it until you make it, it's time for you and I to stand for true deliverance. This is a major problem, especially in the Body of Christ. A lot of folks are wearing a mask for the crowd for validation and accolades. Everyone wants to be liked or seen. Everyone wants a huge membership or to fit in with those who appear to be the big wigs in Christendom. This causes many of us to perpetuate a fraud, which is a mistaken identity that becomes a crisis. We feel the need to keep up with latest fashion, instead of making our own fashion become a statement. We want to drive the best, even if we can't afford it, or live in a big house, so we can appear to the natural eye that we have arrived and we are Mr. or Miss It; however, it's all a lie and one big Masquerade Party. Most are hiding behind the mask, but behind closed doors there's a war going on. You want to show your true self and want to reveal your unique self, but are afraid of being different and possibly laughed at and counted out. When the Father made you, He took one look at you and He said, wow, that's good. It doesn't matter what man may think of you, but what the Father said and thinks of you. We must change our language of how we feel about ourselves. Sometimes we are so worried about man's opinions, until we aren't concerned about the one opinion that matters.

For years, I made decisions and did things based on others. I would always place others before me and my needs. I'd do whatever and it didn't matter if I had anything at all, I just wanted others to like or love me, so I based my life around theirs. Even when it came to working or relocating, I didn't work a certain job or moved, because I was more concerned about the well-being of those I allowed into my personal space and heart. However, now that the Masquerade has been executed, I can reveal the absolute beauty of me like a caterpillar that comes out of the cocoon; the real Latisha Revealed and how beautiful I am! I, as many of you always would say, want to have more of God or to be anointed, but it's a great price to pay for the oil, and you won't just go through one process but there are different levels of anointing that cost much more than the one before. We must remember the process to produce the oil. Without the pressing, there will be no oil. We must remember that trials come to try us and to make us, and the fire comes to burn up those unwanted things that are not the will of God for our lives. The fire helps to mold us, that we will be able to stand firm and not so easily moved. We must remember that we are the clay and God is the potter and without fire we can't become that fine masterpiece, fit for the Master's use. Job said, "But He knows the way that I take; when he had tried me than I shall be as gold."

All that has happened was necessary. You might have endured and suffered much, but glory is approaching quickly. God is about to show you off to the world. You've been in the background and working behind the scenes, but the reward of the unseen, is about to be revealed. Never be ashamed of your past and the unfortunate mishaps that have occurred, no matter what it was. It had to take place, it had to happen and nothing just happens. Your life and my life are predestined before we were even conceived. Before your parents met or before you were placed in a woman's womb or however you may have gotten here on earth, there is a beginning and a final destination, and there's a dash which is the in between time and is full of many disappointments, challenges, circumstances, pain and promise. I'm here to encourage you not to lose the hope of your promise.

Through the many difficulties of my life and everything that has taken place, the good, the bad and the very ugly, it all has and shall continue to serve its purpose. Beloved, just continue to be true to yourself and do everything in your power and in God to stay free. Never allow yourself to be trapped and in a fantasy that you have to place a mask on your face to be important or accepted. Face all of your past obstacles and traumatic events, and deal with all of the new ones that may come up throughout your life. Don't get caught up in the hype; love God and love yourself the way He loves you! You can't even love wholeheartedly if you don't truly love you and who you are. When you look in the mirror every day, make sure you smile and blow a kiss at yourselves. Women and men, you smile and give a thumbs up. Know that you must be all around healthy in order to be successful and help others. If you're feeling down and depressed, deal with it and get help so you can be healed whole. If you don't deal with it and face the facts, that's when you will invite the Masquerade Party in and cover up the real and truly priceless you. People may give up on you, but don't you give up on you!

Beloved, I need you to know that you're not in anything alone, that God will never leave nor forsake you and if you need help on earth, go get help. Don't ever be ashamed to ask for help. Being depressed or trying to commit suicide isn't the answer at all. You are loved more than you know. You're someone's hero or shero. As a matter of a fact, get a paper now and write down all the good things that are occurring right now in your life and then write down all the not so good things that are currently occurring. I can guarantee you that it's not as bad as you think. I'll start your list for you: God woke you up this morning, that's a reason to smile. No matter the struggle, it's a blessing to be above ground and not on a cooling board. Listen, the Glory of God which is shining through us is revealed to us and through us, because we made it this far and we didn't quit, but we keep pressing forward. You, beloved, when you get home or wherever you may be dwelling at, please know that God did what He promised, "He supplied your needs according to his riches and glory." God supplies us daily, not weekly or monthly. He keeps you upright when you are about to trip, and the Holy Ghost comforts you when you are disheartened. God speaks, we just have to be clear minded and attentive to hear and receive what He may be trying to say. Listen closely, it's not always loud, usually it's very soft and gentle to encourage you and to let you know that you can make it.

Are you ready to live and enjoy the rest of life's journey? You need to get excited, because you are revealing your true authentic selves to many. We are about to be that person, that example and light for the world to see. No more delays and procrastination, but holding our heads high and our chest out. Let's do our very best to remain, "steadfast, immovable and always abounding in the works of the Lord, knowing that our labor isn't in vain in the Lord." 1 Corinthians 15:58. Now that we have executed the Masquerade, lights, camera, action; Presenting the real you! The world has been waiting for us and God is redeeming the time for us. He's about to show many, His perfect work in you. No matter what may occur, never ever become bound and entangled with the inner me, which is you that causes a facade and great deceit and false impersonations, to other people.

END TO BEGIN

"Better is the end of a thing than the beginning thereof: and the patient in spirit is better than the proud in spirit."
Ecclesiastes 7:8

There is no chapter thirteen, because chapter twelve is where my life aligned up with the perfect will of God. Spiritually, the number twelve represents, Faith, Perfection of Government, and Divine rule. God has caused the chaos from my past to shake me and has divinely set me in order. Everything that has been out of order is now in order. I have totally without any doubt or reservations given my past, present, and future over to the Father. I've burned the mask and the Father has dumped the ashes into the sea of forgetfulness. I no longer wear the mask of guilt, shame, and pain, it's forever gone and shall never resurface again. God has made me free and I shall remain free.

I'm a firm believer that all endings are better and so much greater than when something first begins. It's great to start a new chapter, but I believe that it's even greater to close the whole book and start a new one. I have closed the old book, to begin a new book and this will be the latter series, of Latisha's life story. Out of all that has occurred I regret none of them, but one thing: that I didn't remove the mask sooner, to reveal my truth and my scars. I hid for years and with doing that held up my own purpose filled with destiny and I believe that I have suffered, because I wouldn't totally surrender to the will of the Father. I didn't give God a total yes and I was afraid of what others would think of me, but at the end of 2018, I had a wakeup call and I repented and I also realized that no one matters but Christ, and He is who holds my future. I also realized, that if I didn't do the work that I was assigned to do I would miss Heaven. We can get so busy helping everyone else's vision and forget about our own mandate, that only we can fulfill and carry out. The end of 2018, I told God yes and I will go forth no matter what anyone might think or say. I do believe that the suffering was for my own good, and it also was good medicine for me and it helped me to become the anointed vessel that I am and will become even more!

Everything that has occurred in my life, is so much more than I could write and place in a book, but I do believe that while time progresses, I will be able to tell more. I believe that my latter life will allow me to be EVERYTHING that God has called me and chosen me to be. YES, I've wasted time and God has been gracious to me, even in all my disobedience and doing what I wanted to do. I ran a long time from doing the perfect will of God, and now that I have totally surrendered, He can perfect the things that concern me and I believe, because of my obedience, that there has been an unlocking for greater and better to occur in my life.

All of it was necessary! I wouldn't be able to help anyone without the overcoming and coming out. I pat myself on the back and encourage myself, that I have made the choice to live totally for God and obey everything the Holy Writ has said. No, it's never easy to say no sometimes, and it's not easy to say yes either, but I promise you all, that I will do my best to please the Father and Him alone in everything I do. I will always give Him all the glory for all He has done for me and what He allows me to do, and the times He has brought me out as well. I won't take or give His glory to anyone. The End to Begin, my new book of my life is so amazing and I'm excited about it. My life is an open book to men and women all around the globe, for them to see me as a holy example and also an example of a proven fact that no matter what your issue might have been, you can start all over again with Jesus and recover all. Shalom. Mega Blessings, God's Servant Daughter.

LATISHA R. MITCHELL

ABOUT THE AUTHOR

ELDER PROPHETESS LATISHA RENE'E MYZICK-MITCHELL

Elder Prophetess Latisha Renee Myzick-Mitchell is a native of Georgetown, South Carolina. She is the eldest of two children. Elder Mitchell was a very unique and peculiar child growing up. In November 1989, with her mother, Evangelist Julia Myzick-Watkins, who was a woman of great inspiration, a demonstrator of holiness and her great mentor spiritually, Elder Mitchell at the age of nine, accepted Jesus as her personal Lord and Savior and received the gift of the Holy Spirit with the evidence of speaking in tongues as the Spirit gave her utterance. As she began to grow in the things of God, Elder

Mitchell began to work in ministry. She began with singing in the choir, then becoming a Praise and Worship Leader at Love Chapel Deliverance Center in Georgetown, under the Leadership of Apostle Richard Frasier and Pastor Avis Frasier, where she also served as Pastor Avis Frasier's armor bearer for nine years. Under this leadership, Elder Mitchell witnessed and learned that to become a servant in the Kingdom is the greatest ministry of all.

After running for many years from the calling to preach the gospel, Elder Mitchell accepted her calling and preached her initial sermon on October 23, 2004, and received her minister/evangelist license. As an evangelist she has several community outreach ministries which are parts of her active ministry: feeding the hungry, prison outreach, and women's ministries.

After being at Love Chapel Deliverance Center for twelve years, the Lord moved Elder Mitchell to join Greater True Light Sounds of Praise on April 15, 2007, and on October 23, 2010 she became an Ordained Elder under the leadership and guidance of the Senior Pastor Bishop Alfred E. Williams.

Elder Mitchell is the founder and current director of the worldwide women's ministry, "Women Beyond the Wall: Women Reaching Women." This ministry was formally established in 2010. Elder Mitchell is dedicated to helping women learn how to live and be holy Women of God. Even though she has been through pain, disappointments, being misunderstood, abused and disliked, because of holiness, she is determined to continue to live as a holy Woman of God. November of 2018, God instructed Elder Mitchell to change the ministry name from "Women Beyond the Walls Worldwide Ministries" to "Beyond The Walls Worldwide Ministries," because God said He wanted Elder Mitchell to not only minister to women, but to women, men and the youth at large.

"Reaching To Restore"

Elder Mitchell has a heart for God's people and will do whatever it takes to reach the lost at any cost. She has a made up mind to tell the truth and to preach God's unadulterated Word. Elder Mitchell also walks in a prophetic anointing and is a latter day Prophet. Her continued desire is to serve and build up; working always to destroy Satan's kingdom; warn the people of God about His coming; and she has been anointed and appointed to preach, teach, reach, and empower women of all generations. Her favorite quote is: "Drive and Go Forward..."

Elder Mitchell graduated from Georgetown High School. She has an Associate's Degree in Criminal Justice from Horry Georgetown Technical College and she has also studied Phlebotomy at Professional Medical Training Center.

Elder Mitchell is a loving mother of two children: A son, Paulzair, 17, and daughter, Promise, 10.

Made in the USA
Middletown, DE
02 April 2021